# BLIZZARDS OF TWEED

## GLEN BAXTER

BLOOMSBURY

Special thanks to :
Sylvie Boulanger, Liz Calder, Jaco Groot,
Polly Napper, Hank Williams & Pascal Yonet

Published by Bloomsbury Publishing, New York and London.
Distributed to the trade by St. Martin's Press

A CIP catalogue record for this book is available from the Library of Congress

ISBN 1 58234 056 0

First U. S. Edition 1999
10 9 8 7 6 5 4 3 2 1

Printed and bound in Great Britain by Butler & Tanner Limited, Frome

# BLIZZARDS, A USER'S GUIDE

Nº 16:   *How to avoid mathematics*

Nº 56: How to floss correctly

№ 153:  How to set a tiger trap

Nº 246:   How to open a door

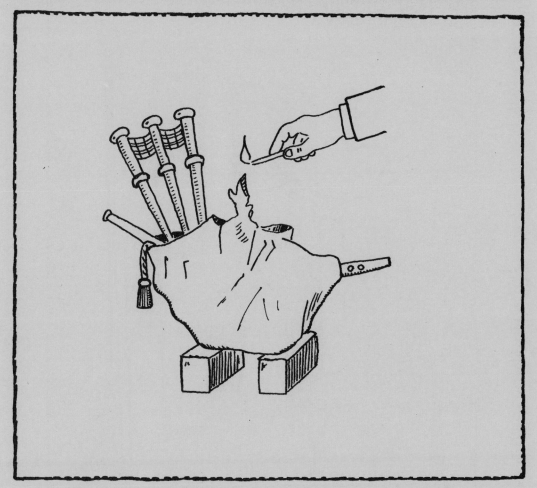

N°14:   *How to appreciate the bagpipes*

WITH THE ADVENT OF SPRING I SET
ABOUT ONE OR TWO MINOR IMPROVEMENTS
TO THE NURSERY

FORTUNATELY ROBIN WAS ON
HAND TO ENSURE MY NEW SCHOOL
UNIFORM WAS A PERFECT FIT

ST. ANSELM'S WAS ALWAYS A
DIFFICULT AWAY FIXTURE

OUR MEETINGS WERE BECOMING MORE
AND MORE EMOTIONALLY CHARGED

OUR RELATIONSHIP SEEMED TO BE
GETTING OFF TO AN UNEASY START

"JUST EXACTLY WHAT IS THIS HOBBY
OF YOURS, CLIVE?" SNAPPED ALICE

TUESDAY EVENINGS WERE SET ASIDE
FOR SEXUAL GRATIFICATION

# TELEPHONE SEX

MANY NEW LINES HAVE BEEN MADE
AVAILABLE TO COPE WITH THE INCREASED
DEMAND FOR THOSE WITH SPECIALIST NEEDS

ONCE I HAD MASTERED THE VOLTAGE CONTROL, I WAS
ABLE TO JOIN TREVOR IN A FRENZY OF ORGASMIC BLISS

AFTER A FEW MONTHS I REALIZED IT
WAS SIMPLY A DEVICE FOR SHOWING
ME HIS THIGHS

"I DO AMUSING THINGS WITH MY EARS"
ANNOUNCED ERIC OMINOUSLY

JULIAN'S EXPLOITS IN THE BOUDOIR
QUICKLY BECAME THE TALK OF PARIS

WHEN IT CAME TO EROTIC FANTASY, TIM
WAS CLEARLY IN A LEAGUE OF HIS OWN

23

DIANE'S FREQUENT ERUPTIONS SOON FORMED
THE BASIS OF A STEADY RELATIONSHIP

THE BILSTAFF BROTHERS WERE ALWAYS ON HAND TO ENSURE MY SHORT STAY AT THE HOTEL MIRAMAR WOULD INDEED BE MEMORABLE

INTERRUPTING HELEN DURING HER LUNCH
BREAK WAS NOT ALWAYS SUCH A GOOD IDEA

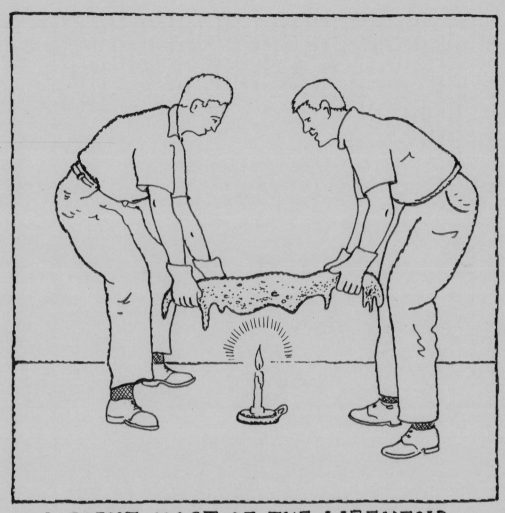

I SPENT MOST OF THE WEEKEND
ASSISTING BRIAN WITH HIS OMELETTES

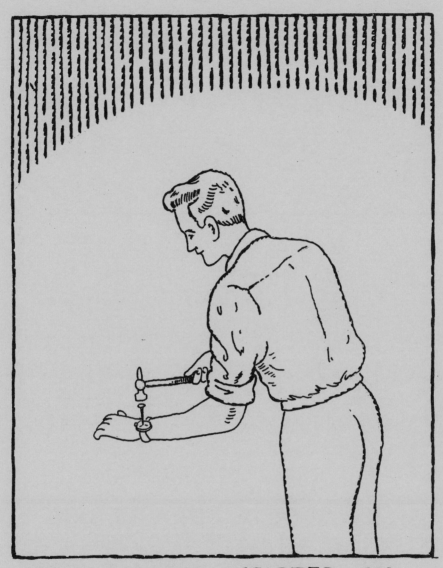

ERIC ALWAYS INSISTED ON
CARRYING OUT HIS OWN REPAIRS

THE DISPOSAL OF BOB'S C.D COLLECTION TOOK A
LITTLE LONGER THAN WE HAD ORIGINALLY THOUGHT

UNFORTUNATELY, FATHER'S LITTLE ECONOMIES
HAD RECENTLY BEEN EXTENDED TO HAIRDRESSING

FOR EIGHT LONG YEARS I STRUGGLED
HARD TO PERFECT OUR LITTLE ACT

JANET DISCOVERED THAT PETTY
NEIGHBOURHOOD DISPUTES WERE QUICKLY
RESOLVED WITH THE ATOMIZER

JANET WAS BACK AND CLEARLY
IN NO MOOD FOR COMPROMISE

INTER-OFFICE COMMUNICATION
SEEMED TO BE WORKING SMOOTHLY

ROBIN NOTICES SOME DISTURBING NEW
DEVELOPMENTS IN THE NEIGHBOURHOOD

# GREAT SPORTING MOMENTS Nº28

"SLOGGER" BLEASDALE'S LAST-MINUTE EQUALISER
DRINDLEMUIR UNITED v BRADTHORPE ROVERS
NOV. 15ᵀᴴ 1956 (Final Score 16~16)

WITHIN A MATTER OF MINUTES WE
WERE GETTING ON FAMOUSLY

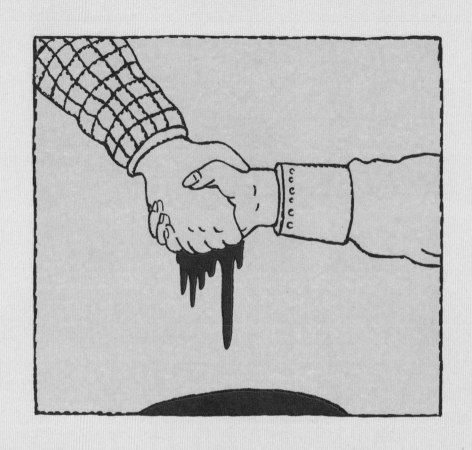

"TOGETHER WE COULD MAKE BEAUTIFUL
OMELETTES" WHISPERED ANGUS

I WAS BEGINNING TO SUSPECT THAT
THE JOB INTERVIEW WAS NOT GOING
AT ALL WELL

"LET ME EXPLAIN HOW THE CENTRAL
HEATING SYSTEM WORKS" ANNOUNCED
OUR JOVIAL LANDLORD

THE REMOVAL OF NIGEL'S MASCARA WAS
ALWAYS A PERILOUS UNDERTAKING

EDWIN'S CAREFULLY PLANNED ROUTE APPEARED
TO BE TAKING US STEADILY UPSTREAM

42

"YOU'D BETTER HAVE A DAMNED GOOD EXCUSE FOR BEING OUT OF UNIFORM THIS TIME, WAINWRIGHT!" BARKED THE SERGEANT

UNCLE EDWIN COULD USUALLY BE RELIED
UPON TO PROVIDE VISITORS WITH A
WELCOME TOUCH OF SOUTHERN HOSPITALITY

AS USUAL, THE BANK MANAGER
SEEMED DELIGHTED TO SEE ME

AS PROMISED, EVERY DAY THAT SUMMER
LYDIA SENT ME FRESH FLOWERS

THE EASTER EGG HUNT AT LOWER CHEDLEY
WAS KNOWN TO BE ONE OF THE TOUGHEST
IN THE WHOLE OF WILTSHIRE

AN EVENING OF DUTCH CULTURE
REMAINED AN OMINOUS POSSIBILITY

BIG CITY DEMAND FOR SUSHI BRINGS ABOUT ONE OR TWO
CHANGES ALONG THE OLD CHISHOLM TRAIL

THERE WERE THOSE WHO FELT THE SECURITY
ARRANGEMENTS FOR BRENDA'S LUNCHBOX
WERE JUST A SHADE EXCESSIVE

THIS SEEMED TO BE THE YEAR WHEN
MY PARENTS AND I WOULD BE
ENJOYING OUR OWN SEPARATE HOLIDAYS

WE SOON SETTLED DOWN INTO THE PACE OF LIFE IN THE BIG CITY

"I FIND MONET ALWAYS PROVIDES SUCH A CHEERY BLAZE" NOTED THE CONNOISSEUR

53

HAPPY HOUR AT PORT DUNCAN SEEMED
TO PASS RELATIVELY SMOOTHLY

I DEFTLY SKETCHED IN THE
FINER POINTS OF MY THESIS

POPULAR DELUSIONS N°26

PETER IMAGINES HE HAS CAUGHT
SIGHT OF THE WAITER

IT LOOKED SUSPICIOUSLY LIKE
A CONTINENTAL BREAKFAST

THERE WAS MUCH TALK IN THE VILLAGE OF
LORD HEMSHAW'S SUDDEN, INEXPLICABLE
INTEREST IN THE WAYS OF MARQUETRY

UNCLE BOB'S TECHNIQUE FOR CATCHING
TROUT WAS SIMPLICITY ITSELF

THERE BEING NO DIRECT FLIGHT I
WAS OBLIGED TO CHANGE AT MELBOURNE

I FOUND MYSELF PLEADING GUILTY TO A MOMENTARY LAPSE OF TASTE BETWEEN DECEMBER 31ST 1969 AND JANUARY 1ST 1980

IN THE MURKY TWILIGHT WORLD OF MALE
JEWELRY, KEVIN REMAINED A POTENT FORCE

"I'M AFRAID YOUR COLLECTION OF PORNOGRAPHY
REGRETFULLY DISPLAYS AT LEAST TWO
GLARING OMISSIONS" NOTED LADY BISWOLD

TEX WAS DEFINITELY DEVELOPING
A TASTE FOR MINOR BONNARDS

"I'M LOOKING FOR THE GRINGO THEY CALL
THE DANDRUFF KID" SNARLED MEXICAN PETE

THE NEW BUFFET SERVICE OVER AT THE
HOWARD PLACE WAS PROVING PERHAPS TO
BE JUST A SHADE TOO POPULAR

TEX INSISTED ON STRICT ENFORCEMENT OF
THE NO-SMOKING POLICY IN THE BUNKHOUSE

## THE CONQUEST OF THE WEST

"SUCH A BREATHTAKING VIEW" MUSED KIT
"THERE MUST BE NEAR ENOUGH PARKING
SPACES FOR 800,000 VEHICLES"

"I THINK I'VE DISCOVERED A FUNDAMENTAL
FLAW IN THE INTERNAL LOGIC OF THIS
HERE PICTURE" DRAWLED THE DEPUTY

THE CONCEPT OF THE DIMMER SWITCH HAD
YET TO REACH THE LAZY K BUNKHOUSE

THE MONTHS OF REHEARSAL HAD PAID
OFF AND AT LAST I HAD BECOME AN
INTEGRAL PART OF THE ACT

THERE WERE THOSE WHO WERE BEGINNING
TO SUSPECT THAT DEAD-EYE McCULLOUGH
MIGHT BE LOSING HIS TOUCH

TED'S FIRST VENTURE INTO THE SPHERE
OF MAGIC REALISM APPEARED TO HAVE
RECEIVED MIXED REVIEWS

HAVING A TRUSTY SCOUT WHO REALLY KNEW THE TERRAIN SOON
HELPED TO DISPEL ALL TRACES OF MY EARLIER SKEPTICISM

INITIAL RESPONSE TO MY WATERCOLOURS
WAS NOT ENTIRELY FAVOURABLE

"O.K, M<sup>c</sup>DRUNDLE, JUST BRING THAT
BAGUETTE DOWN REAL EASY!"
BARKED THE MILLINER

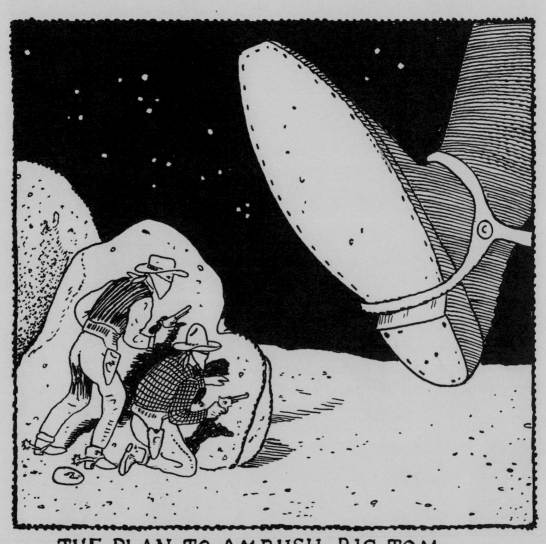

THE PLAN TO AMBUSH BIG TOM
RUNS INTO A SPOT OF TROUBLE

WITH ONE SWIFT AND DECISIVE MOVE
TOM REVEALED THE ILLICIT KUMQUATS

79

"NOW JUST SETTLE DOWN AND RELAX WHILE
I TREAT YOU TO AN EVENING OF MY
FAVOURITE LIMERICKS" BEAMED THOMAS

Nº 26   The Alpine Omelette

LIFE AS A VEGAN IN ROBIN'S BAND
OF MERRIE MEN WAS NOT ALWAYS
JUST A BOWL OF CHERRIES

"JUST RELAX. THERE'S NO DANGER OF
MRS. OMERGHAST DROPPING IN JUST YET"
ANNOUNCED THE AMBASSADOR

THERE WERE THOSE WHO FELT THAT
ROBIN'S DEEP AFFECTION FOR SHERWOOD
WAS JUST A SHADE UNHEALTHY

84

"IN TRUTH THOU DOST FASHION THE MEANEST MARTINI IN THE WHOLE OF NOTTINGHAMSHIRE!" ROARED SIR EDMUND

WITH DEADLY ACCURACY YOUNG SILBURN
PICKED OUT THE WOODPECKER

"DO YOU SUPPOSE A DRY SHERRY WOULD BE OUT
OF THE QUESTION, FORBES?" QUERIED EDWARDES

I REALIZED I HAD PROBABLY BEEN POSTED TO THE MOST
HEAVILY EXPLORED REGION EAST OF NEWPORT PAGNELL

"RUMOUR HAS IT YOU'VE BEEN TRANSFERRED
TO INTELLIGENCE, SNEDLEY"

WE MADE OUR WAY UP THROUGH
CONTEMPORARY FICTION AND ON
TO THE CAPUCCINO MACHINE

UNFORTUNATELY, BRENDA'S VISITS WERE
BECOMING MORE AND MORE FREQUENT

STANDARDS OF ORDER AND HARMONY
WERE PURSUED WITH UNPRECEDENTED
VIGOUR ON THE ESTATE OF LORD WILMHURST

I NOTED A RAPID DETERIORATION IN
THE TONE OF THE TOURNAMENT

WORK ON THE RIETVELD BIDET
CONTINUED LONG INTO THE NIGHT

THE NEW ACCOUNTANT SEEMED DETERMINED
TO CREATE A LASTING IMPRESSION ON
HIS FIRST DAY WITH THE PARTNERSHIP

"PERHAPS THIS WILL HELP YOU TO
APPRECIATE THE SOARING LYRICAL
BEAUTY OF MY POEMS" ANNOUNCED
THE AUTHOR DECISIVELY